Jellyfish Can't Swim

and Other Secrets from the Animal World

by Marjorie Hodgson Parker

Chariot Books™
David C. Cook Publishing Co.

With all my love and thanks to God and my family—
especially Mom and Dad.

Chariot Books™ is an imprint of David C. Cook Publishing Co.
David C. Cook Publishing Co., Elgin, Illinois 60120
David C. Cook Publishing Co., Weston, Ontario
Nova Distribution LTD., Torquay, England

JELLYFISH CAN'T SWIM AND OTHER SECRETS FROM THE
ANIMAL WORLD

Edited by Lois Keffer
Book and cover design by Tim Davis
Illustrations by Tim Davis

First printing, 1991
Printed in the United States of America
95 94   5 4

Verses marked (NIV) are taken from the Holy Bible, New International Version.
Copyright© 1973,1978,1984, International Bible Society.

Verses marked (TLB) are taken from The Living Bible© 1971, owned by assign-
ment by Illinois Regional Bank N.A. (as trustee). Used by permission of Tyndale
House Publishers Inc., Wheaton, IL 60189. All rights reserved.

Library of Congress Cataloging-in-Publication Data

Parker, Marjorie Hodgson.
    Jellyfish can't swim and other secrets from the animal world / by
Marjorie Hodgson Parker.
        p. cm.
    Summary: Highlights the habits and behavior of a variety of animals,
and suggests ways to conduct oneself at home, at school, and at church
in order to glorify God. Includes scriptures and prayers.
    ISBN 1-55513-393-2:
    1. Children—Prayer-books and devotions—English. 2. Animals—
Religious aspects—Christianity—Juvenile literature. [1. Prayer
books and devotions. 2. Animals—Habits and behavior. 3. Christian
life. 4. Conduct of life.] I. Title. II. Title: Jellyfish can't swim.
BV4870.P36   1991
242'.62—dc20   91-3236
                                                               CIP
                                                               AC

Solomon, who was the wisest of kings,
Noticed the habits of many small things.
In Proverbs, he spoke of the wise ways of creatures.
King Solomon thought even ants were good teachers!
Habits of creatures both great and small
Teach loving lessons of God to us all.

THE FRIENDLY ELEPHANT

Would you like to have a friend who acts like an elephant? Maybe you didn't know it, but elephants know how to be good friends. And they do it naturally, without anyone telling them what to do.

If an elephant is sick or hurt, he is often too weak to get to the watering hole. But his friends come to help. Two of them will get beside him (one on each side) and hold him up with their strong bodies as he walks. Then he can get a drink at the watering hole and cool off. Often another elephant will come over to stroke the sick elephant with her trunk.

You don't have a trunk, of course, but you have hands to place a cool wash cloth on a sick person's head, or to bring a drink of water. You can send a get well card or a funny book. Then you'll be showing love the way Jesus did. We're doing God's work when we help and comfort each other.

SCRIPTURE: *I needed clothes and you clothed me, I was sick and you looked after me, I was in prison and you came to visit me.*
Matthew 25:36, NIV

REMEMBER: Elephant "nurses" know just what to do. To help sick friends feel good as new. Like friendly elephants, you can help too.

WHEN YOU PRAY: Ask God to help you be like a friendly elephant when someone is sick.

WALL OF HORNS

Some animals know how to protect the weaker members of their group. Certain reindeer have a special way of guarding their friends. When wolves attack, the strong ones make a circle around the ones that need protection. There may be young ones who haven't had a chance to grow their horns yet, or some old, frail reindeer whose horns are broken.

Sometimes reindeer run in circles and make a whirling wall of horns so the wolves can't get inside. The wolves finally get tired of waiting and go away.

When people are scared and worried, they need help just like the reindeer. You can help by standing up for them when others are being mean. You can be friendly. You can pray for them. Christians can stand together against trouble.

SCRIPTURE: *Finally, be strong in the Lord and in his mighty power. Put on the full armor of God so that you can take your stand against the devil's schemes.   Ephesians 6:10, 11, NIV.*

REMEMBER: If you pray for friends when something goes wrong,
And show them God's love, you help them along.
With God and each other, we stand, and we're strong.

WHEN YOU PRAY: Think of someone who seems sad or worried and ask God to help that person.

Purr-fect Praise

When you stroke a kitten or a cat, you usually "start its motor." The whole cat seems to vibrate when it purrs, doesn't it? Because it is purring, you know it's very happy. Even if you can't hear the little sound it's making, you can feel it. It makes you want to keep stroking the cat, too!

The cat, in its own way, is saying, "Thank you. That feels good." He is praising you in cat language!

God "strokes" us every day with blessings. He likes it when His people praise Him, too.

When you feel good and healthy, when you smell something delicious (like a rose or cookies baking), when you see a beautiful sunset, when you taste your favorite food, when you hear birds singing or music playing, when someone hugs you—that is the time for you to purr and say, "Thank you, God."

> **SCRIPTURE:** *Let everyone bless God and sing his praises, for he holds our lives in his hands. Psalm 66:8, 9a, TLB*
>
> **REMEMBER:** Cats like to purr their thanks to you—
> If you praise God, you thank Him, too.
>
> **WHEN YOU PRAY:** Think of some of your favorite things and thank God for them.

Egg on His Feet

Emperor Penguins live in an icy world. Because they don't build nests, the daddy has a special job.

As soon as the mother penguin lays an egg, the father puts it on top of his feet. That keeps it off the cold ice, so it won't freeze. The daddy has a special fold of skin that hangs down and covers the egg like a warm comforter.

The penguin daddy can't walk around with the egg on his feet, so he just stands there, week after week, for two whole months! He doesn't even eat during that time. He just patiently holds the egg and protects it. When the little penguin is hatched, the mother comes back to take care of it. Then the hungry father can go get something to eat!

Sometimes, like that daddy penguin, you have to do something that takes a lot of time and patience. It might be homework, or doing chores, or learning Bible verses. And sometimes you'd rather be out playing!

But take a lesson from the Emperor penguin, and try to do your job without complaining. Like the penguin, you'll be rewarded some day for your patience.

SCRIPTURE: *Let us not get tired of doing what is right, for after a while we will reap a harvest of blessing if we don't get discouraged and give up. Galatians 6:9, TLB*

REMEMBER: If you can be patient like a Penguin Pop
And do what is right, you'll come out on top.

WHEN YOU PRAY: Ask God's help to patiently do what's right.

DANCING ON AIR

Animals and insects "talk" to each other in ways that may seem strange to us. They have their own kinds of language.

Some bees have a language of "dance." Worker bees fly out to find nectar from flowers. They need the nectar for making honey. When they find it, they come back to the hive to tell the other bees about it. They want to share the good news!

The bees spread the word with a special "dance." They make a pattern in the air as they fly, almost like drawing a map. They spin in a small circle—in a round dance—if the food is close by. If it is far away, they show by their movements in the air which direction to go.

You don't have to dance in circles to talk to others. You have lots of ways to communicate, and some really good news to tell. God wants everyone to know how much He loves them. Whether you use words or actions, you can lead others to Jesus, just like bees lead each other to nectar.

How about inviting a friend to Sunday school? Or promising to pray for someone who's in trouble? You can share the good news of how Jesus loves us and forgives us.

SCRIPTURE: *Give thanks to the Lord, call on his name; make known among the nations what he has done. Sing to him, sing praise to him; tell of all his wonderful acts.* *Psalm 105:1, 2, NIV*

REMEMBER: To lead a friend to Jesus,
You need not dance on air.
Your words and deeds can tell about
Jesus' love and care.

WHEN YOU PRAY: Ask God to help you lead others to Him.

WASHED AND DRIED

Did you know that a jellyfish can't swim? It just floats along in the sea, catching food in the long thread-like "legs" that trail behind it. Since it can only float, the jellyfish has to go wherever the current takes it. And sometimes the current takes it where it doesn't want to go!

When a jellyfish gets washed up on the sand, it becomes totally helpless. Since it can't move to get back into the water, the jellyfish just dries up and dies there on the beach.

We can learn a lesson from the "wishy-washy" jellyfish. Sometimes Christians "float" along with the crowd and do what others are doing, just because that's the easy thing to do. The Bible tells us not to go along with others just because "everybody's doing it." We need to do what the Bible says is right, even if it means swimming against the tide.

If you go God's way, you won't end up washed up, dried up, and out of luck. God's way is best, even if you have to go it alone.

SCRIPTURE: *Don't copy the behavior and customs of this world, but be a new and different person with a fresh newness in all you do and think. Then you will learn from your own experience how his ways will really satisfy you.*
Romans 12:2, TLB

REMEMBER: A jellyfish just floats along,
Til it's washed up on the sand.
If you will "swim" and go God's way,
You'll like the place you land!

WHEN YOU PRAY: Ask God to help you go His way, even when others don't.

HELP!

Have you ever heard an egg cry for help? Probably not—but it does happen.

A baby alligator grows inside an egg until it's ready to hatch. Then, if it has trouble breaking out of the shell, the baby alligator cheeps loudly. The baby reptile knows that its cries will bring help. When the mother alligator hears it calling, she comes to the rescue and helps break open the shell.

Helpless animal babies cry in order to bring their parents running (or swimming or flying) to take care of them. Human babies do the same thing.

But it's not just little babies who need help. Everyone needs help lots of times. And God is the best help. Our cry to God for help is usually in prayer. He tells us that when we pray, He will listen. Our Heavenly Father is always ready and willing to help when we are frightened or in trouble.

SCRIPTURE: *You will call upon me and come and pray to me, and I will listen to you. You will seek me and find me when you seek me with all your heart.*
Jeremiah 29:12, 13, NIV

REMEMBER: Animal babies can cheep, cry, or yelp. But God says that prayer is His people's best help.

WHEN YOU PRAY: Thank God for listening to your prayers and for helping you.

FEATHERED FRIENDS

Watch the sky sometime. You might see birds flying and landing together in flocks that look like floating clouds. You might see a long row of birds perched side by side on a telephone wire. In the fall, you could see geese following each other in a "V" shape on their way south.

Birds have lots of ways of helping each other. Crows act as look-outs for other crows. Cedar waxwings pass berries to each other. Apostle birds live and work together in groups of twelve.

Weaverbirds enjoy being together so much that they build "apartments" under one big roof. Working together, they all help weave one big tent-like roof. Then each family of weaverbirds builds its own nest under that roof.

God wants his people to work together and get along with each other like these feathered friends do. You can be a kind, thoughtful neighbor at home or at school—or even when you're walking down the street!

SCRIPTURE: *The entire law is summed up in a single command: "Love your neighbor as yourself."* *Galatians 5:14, NIV*

REMEMBER: Birds help each other avoid hurt and harm,
They follow the leader, and sound the alarm.
They pass along berries, and share spots
of rest.
Let's all be good neighbors. God says
that's best.

WHEN YOU PRAY: Thank God for neighbors and friends, and ask
Him to help you get along with them.

THE PORCUPINE'S PRICKLY PRESERVER

A porcupine looks like a walking pin cushion. Its pins are 30,000 sharp quills. No one wants to pet a porcupine!

The porcupine doesn't have soft fur like most animals, but God gave him those quills for good reasons. If another animal tries to hurt the porcupine, he can use his quills to stab the attacker and make it run away (with a sore nose)!

The porcupine's quills are so light they act like a life-preserver in the water. They make it easy for him to stay afloat as he swims. Those same prickly quills act as a cushion for the porcupine if he falls out of a tree.

God doesn't make all animals or their coverings alike. God doesn't make all people alike, either. People come in all different colors, sizes and shapes. We can thank God for the ways we are alike and the ways we are different.

Most of all, thank God that He has a special place in his plan for you!

SCRIPTURE: *Know that the Lord is God. It is he who made us, and we are his; we are his people, the sheep of his pasture. Psalm 100:3, NIV*

REMEMBER: No matter what you look like
God made you specially you!
Unique for some good purpose,
You're God's great artwork, too!

WHEN YOU PRAY: Ask God to show you special ways you can serve Him.

A FLIP OF THE TONGUE

Have you ever seen a fat frog who looks like he's sitting around doing nothing? If a fly happens to land nearby, that lazy-looking frog suddenly zips out his tongue and snatches the fly so fast you can hardly see it. The frog has a very long tongue just for this purpose. He usually keeps it rolled inside his mouth. But when an insect flies by, he can flip out his tongue quick as a wink and catch a tasty dinner.

The frog knows when to use his tongue and when to sit quietly. His good aim keeps him full and happy. He helps people, too, by getting rid of many bothersome insects.

People's tongues aren't nearly as long as the frog's. And we don't use our tongues to catch insects, but we do use them to catch people's attention with the words we say.

Our words can make a big difference—either for good or bad. God knows that, and in the Bible He explains that we need to control our tongues and watch what we say. Use your words to encourage people. Telling a friend what you like about him or her. If you say the wrong things and hurt someone's feelings, you can always use your tongue to make things right by saying, "I'm sorry."

SCRIPTURE: *Self-control means controlling the tongue! A quick retort can ruin everything.*
Proverbs 13:3, TLB

REMEMBER: A frog can control his tongue well
And uses it just as he should.
If you can control your tongue, too,
The Bible says that's very good!

WHEN YOU PRAY: Ask God to help you use your tongue in helpful ways.

SWIMMING ALONG, SINGING A SONG

How big is big? Some whales are larger than three school buses parked end to end! Their brains are so big that scientists believe whales may be very smart, too. People who study whales have learned that they pass on what they know by singing to each other. Their tunes are not like our songs, and people can't understand them. But to the whales, the songs are full of meaning.

Whale songs are passed from mother or father to their baby whales. A grandfather whale may sing a song to his grandson to teach him something as they swim along. The little whale memorizes it and then passes it on.

People pass along stories and songs to each other, too. God gave His story to men to write down and pass along. We can find these wonderful stories in the Bible. God tells His people to continue to pass along the good news in His Word. You can do that by telling a friend a Bible story, talking about God's love, or passing on a song you learned at church.

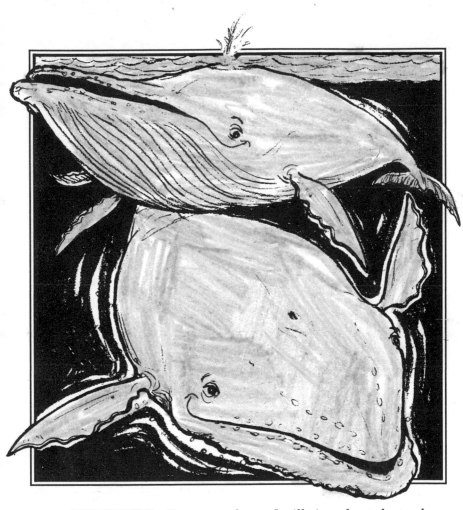

SCRIPTURE: *Forever and ever I will sing about the tender kindness of the Lord! Young and old shall hear about your blessings.   Psalm 89:1, TLB*

REMEMBER: Whales sing a song while they're swimming along
To pass lessons on to the rest.
You've got the Word, so tell what you've heard.
The Bible's Good News is the best.

WHEN YOU PRAY: Thank God for His Word, the Bible.

Cub Rub-a-Dub

Have you ever seen a picture of a mother lion licking her cub? That's how she washes it clean. It's also how she shows her love for her cub. The baby will lick its mother, too, in order to show its love back to her.

Jesus proved His love for us by washing us clean in a very different way. He made a way for us to be clean on the *inside*. When He died on the cross, He took the punishment that we deserve for wrong things we have done. Jesus says He will forgive us if we believe in Him and ask forgiveness. Like the mother lion, Jesus washes us clean over and over.

Once we are forgiven, Jesus wants us to turn around and forgive other people, too. That's one way we can show our love for Him.

SCRIPTURE: *For if you forgive men when they sin against you, your heavenly Father will also forgive you.   Matthew 6:14, NIV*

REMEMBER: With her tongue, not a tub, a mom cleans her cub
And the cub learns from her what to do.
With forgiveness of sins, through Christ we are cleansed.
In return, we forgive others, too.

WHEN YOU PRAY: Think of someone you need to forgive, and ask God to help you do it.

TRACKS!

If you walk along a sandy road or look in a mud puddle that's drying up, you might see the impression of a bird's footprints or a dog's tracks, or maybe even the tracks of a raccoon or possum. Funny shapes and sizes of footprints show what kinds of creatures have been there.

You can tell where people have been, too, by the impression they leave behind. People leave "footprints" with more than just their feet. The words we say can stick in someone's mind like footprints in drying mud. The things we do leave an imprint, too.

Our tracks show others what kind of people we are. If we walk as Jesus walked, others will know we are Christians. His way was one of kindness and love.

You can leave footprints of kindness and love by going to a nursing home to cheer up a lonely person. Or going to a neighbor's house to deliver a picture you have drawn for them, or a cheerful note and a flower. Your loving tracks can lead others to Jesus.

SCRIPTURE: *He will teach the ways that are right and best to those who humbly turn to him. And when we obey him, every path he guides us on is fragrant with his lovingkindness and his truth. Psalm 25:9, 10, TLB*

REMEMBER: God's creatures leave prints as they run, walk, or play.
Your tracks can lead others to walk in God's way.

WHEN YOU PRAY: Ask God to help you do nice things so you can leave Christian "tracks."

HEAD HOWLER

Did you know that some monkeys howl? They're named Howling Monkeys for their loud screams. Although they can make a lot of noise, howling monkeys like peace. They howl to scare away enemies so they won't have to fight.

These monkeys don't fight over who gets to be leader in their group, either. They peacefully take turns being "head monkey." Each monkey is as important as the others in their group.

The monkeys don't know it, but they are acting the way the Bible tells people to act (except for the howling, of course!). Jesus said not to argue over who gets to be the most important. He wants us to let others go ahead of us. To be truly great in God's eyes, we need to learn how to serve others.

SCRIPTURE: *The greatest among you will be your servant. For whoever exalts himself will be humbled, and whoever humbles himself will be exalted.   Matthew 23:31, NIV*

REMEMBER: Aiming to be "most important" on earth
Does not have any heavenly worth.
Don't push and shove to be Number One,
Be kind and serve, as did God's Son.

WHEN YOU PRAY: Ask God to help you serve others happily.

BEASTS OF BURDEN

People of different countries chose various animals to be load-carriers because of their strength. These animals are called "beasts of burden." They help by carrying loads that people aren't strong enough to carry alone.

Some of the beasts of burden are big animals. Some are rather small, like the Eskimo dogs called Huskies. Huskies pull heavy sleds across ice and through frozen snow. One Huskie alone couldn't pull a very heavy load. But when the dogs work together in teams, they are very strong, because each one helps the others.

Even huge animals like oxen often work together, joined by a yoke, which is something like a big wooden collar. Pulling side by side, they are twice as strong as one alone would be.

Sometimes being worried or scared about something can feel like a burden—a heavy weight that seems to pull you down. Jesus said if you pray to God in His name for help, He will make your burden lighter. He'll help you feel better.

Jesus wants to be on the same team with you. He wants to be "yoked" to you, helping you, making you stronger.

SCRIPTURE: *Come to me, all you who are weary and burdened, and I will give you rest. Take my yoke upon you and learn from me, for I am gentle and humble and you will find rest for your souls.* *Matthew 11:28, 29, NIV*

REMEMBER: When you're scared or sad, you don't feel strong.
But Jesus has promised to help you along.
He's strong and can help you do your best,
He'll give you peace and help you rest.

WHEN YOU PRAY: Share with God whatever is bothering you.

TOP JOB

If you worked inside a honey bee hive, you'd see lots of busy bees! But they're not all making honey. Some are builders, putting together little rooms to store the honey. Other bees guard the stored honey. Some are baby sitters, taking care of the baby bees. "Chef" bees are cooks who make "beebread" to feed the baby bees.

Some bees fan their wings to keep the hive cool. The bees you see buzzing around flowers are nectar gatherers.

One bee is the queen. She has lots of servants who wash and comb and feed her. She lays eggs that hatch into baby bees so the hive will stay full of workers.

It takes all kinds of bees to do the many jobs that make a hive work. And it takes all kinds of people and talents to do God's work here on earth. Not every job seems to be a "top job," and not everyone can be a queen bee.

But God has an important job for each of us. It is the task of serving Him. One way to serve Him is by being kind—maybe asking a shy schoolmate to join a game, or by helping your mom or dad. Whatever your task, if you do it for God, it's a "top job."

SCRIPTURE: *Just as there are many parts to our bodies, so it is with Christ's body. We are all parts of it, and it takes every one of us to make it complete, for we each have different work to do. So we belong to each other, and each needs all the others.*   Romans 12:4, 5, TLB

REMEMBER: Like buzzing bees we have jobs to do.
Each job's important. God counts on you.

WHEN YOU PRAY: Ask God to show you ways you can serve Him.

GIFT STICKS

Animals don't celebrate Christmas and other special days. But sometimes they do give each other gifts. A crow brings sticks to his favorite girlfriend. She uses them in her nest to make it strong.

A boy penguin gives pebbles to his girlfriend. She builds a place that helps keep cold wind off her eggs.

Wolf spiders bring food gifts, and boy dance flies bring their girlfriends balloons of silk.

When these creatures give gifts, they show their female friends that they are special. By making a present for a friend or someone in your family, you can show how much you love that person. It doesn't matter what the gift is. In fact, your gift could be just spending some time with a lonely person. Or it could be a note, a card, or even just a smile.

SCRIPTURE: ". . . We must help the weak, remembering the words the Lord Jesus himself said: 'It is more blessed to give than to receive.' " Acts 20:35b, NIV

REMEMBER: As a stick or stone can be a bird's prize, Your smile is a gift in another's eyes.

WHEN YOU PRAY: Each morning ask God to help you give a loving surprise to someone.

ANIMAL TOOLS

A sea otter's dinner is often a mollusk—a sea food dinner inside a hard shell. The otter "sets its table" not with a knife or fork, but with a rock. It makes a table out of its chest.

The otter floats on its back, balancing the rock on its chest. Then it takes the mollusk and pounds the hard shell on the rock until the shell breaks open. The otter then eats the meat inside.

The otter is using the rock as a tool to help him get the food he needs.

God gives people a tool too. It is the Bible. It was written by special men God chose. Believers have used it for thousands of years. The Bible helps us know God better and understand how He wants us to live. It also cheers us up when we're afraid, and tells us all about God's wonderful promises.

SCRIPTURE: *Open my eyes to see wonderful things in your Word. Psalm 119:18, TLB*

REMEMBER: The Bible is God's tool for you—
It tells you the right things to do,
And all about God's promises, too.

WHEN YOU PRAY: Thank God for His tool, the Bible.

HIGH JUMPER

Do you know which of God's creatures is the best jumper? You can't see his muscles. In fact, you can barely see **him**! If you have a dog or cat, you might have seen one of these jumpers. Can you guess? It's a flea! If you could jump as high as a flea can for his size, you could leap clear over a tall building.

God gives special skills to even the tiniest of creatures. The animals use their talents and do their best without even thinking about it. People need to use the talents God gives them, too. It's easy to think you're too weak or too small or too shy to matter. Some people think they are not smart enough to do anything special.

But look at the flea! No matter what size or shape you are, God made you able to do something well. With time and practice, you can find out what you do best. Then do it joyfully, to help others and to honor God.

SCRIPTURE: *God has given each of you some special abilities; be sure to use them to help each other, passing on to others God's many kinds of blessings.   1 Peter 4:10, TLB*

REMEMBER: You have a talent like the tiny flea,
But if you don't know just what it might be,
Ask God to show you. And then you'll see!

WHEN YOU PRAY: Ask God to help you find out what you do best.

THE SPIDER WEB SECRET

Have you ever accidently walked into a spider web and had it stick to your face? The spider makes its web sticky so that it can catch bugs for dinner. Did you ever wonder how the spider keeps from getting stuck in its own trap?

There's a secret to a spider's web. The spider makes *some* strands that are not sticky, just for itself. It only walks along those dry strands. By staying on the right path, the spider doesn't get stuck.

The Bible tells us how to choose the best path in our lives. It says "Mark out a straight and smooth path for your feet so that those who follow you . . . will not fall." (Heb. 12:13) One way to make a straight path is to tell the truth. Being honest isn't always easy, but it's always the right thing to do. And it will keep you from getting stuck in a lie.

SCRIPTURE: *Your word is a lamp to my feet and a light for my path.   Psalm 119:105, NIV*

REMEMBER: Spiders make a secret path
To take them on their way.
Make your path straight with honest words,
And walk in truth each day.

WHEN YOU PRAY: Ask God to help you tell the truth—even when it's hard.

THE FAT ANT

Have you ever watched an ant carry away a piece of food? Sometimes the food is bigger than the ant! It's fun to watch ants scurrying this way and that, looking for food and bringing it back to the nest. But there's one ant who doesn't run around. His job is to store food in his body for other ants.

This ant eats honey until it is stuffed so tight it becomes as round as a tiny balloon. Then it goes underground into the ant tunnels. The fat ant attaches itself to the top of a tunnel, and spends the rest of its life hanging there, feeding other ants. Hungry ants who pass under that live "honeypot" can reach up and get a drink of honey whenever they need it.

God tells His people to feed the hungry, too. But not like that! You can share what you have by giving some of your allowance to help feed the poor. Or you can collect cans of food to give to a place that takes care of hungry people.

SCRIPTURE: *For I was hungry and you gave me something to eat, I was thirsty and you gave me something to drink, I was a stranger and you invited me in.*
Matthew 25:35, NIV

REMEMBER: The lesson we learn from an ant honeypot Is to help feed the hungry, as Jesus taught.

WHEN YOU PRAY: Thank God for the food you eat and ask Him to help you find a way to share food with hungry people.

"Killer" Whale

Have you ever heard of killer whales? They got that name because some folks thought they would kill anything, even people.

But after scientists caught a killer whale to study it, they found out they had been wrong. They found that a killer whale can be very affectionate. A famous whale named Namu liked to have his tummy rubbed and his nose scratched.

Namu's owner, Mr. Griffin, fed him 400 pounds of fish a day. One day he decided to go for a swim with Namu. When Mr. Griffin jumped into the water, Namu rushed over and carried him back to the dock. Namu thought his owner had accidentally fallen in the pool!

Killer whales like Namu once were thought to be mean, but people found out they weren't mean at all. Sometimes we are too quick to think we know what other **people** are like, too. We could be wrong. Jesus warned not to judge others. Give people a chance. You'll probably find out that they're pretty nice after all!

SCRIPTURE: *Do not judge, and you will not be judged. Do not condemn, and you will not be condemned. Forgive, and you will be forgiven.*
Luke 6:37, NIV

REMEMBER: Namu was a nice friendly whale all along— So don't you judge others, for you could be wrong.

WHEN YOU PRAY: Ask God to help you look for the good in others.

Storing What's Important

You've probably watched a squirrel busily scurrying up and down tree trunks. Sometimes you'll see one sitting and nibbling a nut, with its long, bushy tail curling up behind. But do you know what squirrels do when they're not eating or searching for food? They keep busy hiding their food treasures. They bury the nuts in a secret place so they will have plenty to eat in the cold winter months ahead.

Just like squirrels, people need food, too. But we also need a special kind of food that we can't buy at the grocery store. Jesus says we need "food" for the **spirit** that makes us strong **inside** where we think and feel. That kind of food comes from God's Word, the Bible. It is the most important kind of food to store—not in our stomachs, but in our minds and hearts.

You can feed your spirit by reading the Bible or listening to Bible stories. You can "store up" that food by memorizing some verses that make you feel better. Then during times when you feel sad or alone, you can bring out those words you stored away, just as a squirrel feeds on its hidden nuts.

SCRIPTURE: *But Jesus told him, "No! For the Scriptures tell us that bread won't feed men's souls: obedience to every word of God is what we need." Matthew 4:4, TLB*

REMEMBER: Like squirrels storing food before winter's start,
Store up God's word in your mind and your heart.

WHEN YOU PRAY: Ask God to help you memorize a favorite Bible Verse.

STRANGE COMPANIONS

In the animal kingdom, lots of creatures make unlikely friends. A little tickbird rides all day on a big rhinoceros's back, eating the bugs off him. If an enemy tries to sneak up, the bird (who can see a lot better than the rhino) screeches out a warning to his big companion.

A crocodile has a bird friend, too, called a "thick-knee." The crocodile lets the thick-knee walk right into his big toothy mouth to eat the leeches there. He never chomps down on his little friend. And in **that** place, the bird friend is safe from all its enemies while it eats.

When people join together as friends, we can help each other, too—even if we're as different as a rhino, a crocodile and a bird. Church is one place Christians team up in Jesus' name to make good things happen.

One way you can join with others to do good things for Jesus is by encouraging your friends in Sunday school class to save their money for a special missions project. One person alone might not have enough to help, but the offerings of several people can add up to enough to make a difference.

SCRIPTURE: *In response to all he has done for us, let us outdo each other in being helpful and kind to each other and in doing good.*
Hebrews 10:24, TLB

REMEMBER: The rhino and gater team up with some birds.
We Christians can use teamwork, too.
With friends who will help us, it's easy to see
That together, there's lots we can do.

WHEN YOU PRAY: Ask God to help you make the right friends, so together you can do things for Him.

WHY BEARS DON'T FLY

Have you ever seen a bear try to fly? Or have you heard of ducks hiberating all winter in a cave? Of course not! Bears don't try to be ducks and ducks don't try to be bears. They are happy being just what God made them.

A bear learns how to climb trees and catch fish and hibernate by watching its parents. A duck watches its parents, too, and learns to swim and dive and fly. Little animals need their parents to teach them things, just as little people do.

God says it is especially important for children to pay attention to their parents. One of the Ten Commandments says "honor your father and mother." You can honor your parents by obeying quickly and by helping around the house. When you honor your earthly parents, you bring honor to your heavenly Father as well.

SCRIPTURE: *Children, obey your parents in the Lord, for this is right. "Honor your father and mother"—which is the first commandment with a promise—"that it may go well with you and that you may enjoy long life on the earth."* Ephesians 6:1-3, NIV

REMEMBER: Animals watch what ther moms and dads do;
By obeying your parents, you'll honor them, too.

WHEN YOU PRAY: Thank God for your parents and ask Him to help you obey them.

FILL 'ER UP

In the hottest part of the desert, during the hottest time of the year, a camel might not take a drink of water for a week or more. In the winter, a camel can go six **months** without drinking. But after that, our funny-faced, hump-backed animal friend gets very thirsty! Then it can drink as much as three bathtubs full of water in one day. Most people think a camel stores water in his hump. But he doesn't—he stores it in his stomach.

People get thirsty much faster than camels do. And even if we get a big drink, we're thirsty again before long. But Jesus knew that people were also "thirsty" for God's love and forgiveness. He talked about giving people "living water." He meant that if we believe in Him, we'll never be thirsty for God's love again.

If you've never asked Jesus into your heart, you can do it now. He is ready to fill you up with His love and joy.

SCRIPTURE: *Jesus answered, "Everyone who drinks this water will be thirsty again, but whoever drinks the water I give him will never thirst. Indeed, the water I give him will become in him a spring of water welling up to eternal life." John 4:13-14, NIV*

REMEMBER: One drink takes a camel a long way, it's true, When the dry sand grows hotter and hotter. Jesus can give us a drink that lasts, too. His love is our "living water."

WHEN YOU PRAY: Thank God for the love and joy He gives us.

WHAT'S NEW?

Have you ever found an insect's shell, with no bug inside, stuck to a tree trunk? If so, you might have found a cicada's cast-off skin. A baby cicada lives underground for 17 years before it finally digs its way out. Then it finds a tree, climbs it, and begins shedding its old skin.

Maybe you've found a snake skin somewhere. Some insects and creatures (like the snake) grow too big for their old skin and simply crawl out of it.

In fact, some insects become "new creatures." They don't just shed their old skins—their bodies change completely!

Have you ever found an empty cocoon? A caterpillar used to be in there. But by the time it came out, it had turned into a butterfly.

And did you know that the firefly who blinks his "tail light" at you on a summer's night used to be a glow worm?

Unlike an insect, you can never actually shed your skin. But you can shed bad habits and change them to good ones. In the Bible, Paul told people they could become "new creatures" by accepting Jesus into their hearts.

SCRIPTURE: *If anyone is in Christ, he is a new creation;*
the old has gone, the new has come!
2 Corinthians 5:17, NIV

REMEMBER: Is there a bad habit that you need to break?
You can change it to good, for Jesus's sake.
Then see what a lovely "new creature"
you make!

WHEN YOU PRAY: Ask God to help you break a bad habit.

DRUMMER WITH A BEAK

There's one kind of bird who can't sing—but you can still hear it! It talks by hammering on wood with its beak. Do you know which bird it is?

It's the woodpecker. Sometimes he pecks underneath the bark of a tree to find worms and bugs. But most of the time, he uses his hammering to "talk" to other birds. He tells girl birds he is looking for a mate. He also rat-a-tat-tats to tell other male birds that this territory belongs to him.

It doesn't bother the woodpecker that he can't sing. He doesn't worry about what he can't do. He just does what he can with all his might. His pecking can be heard almost a mile away!

People are as different as birds. We don't all have the same talents. Have you ever wished you could do something as well as someone else? When you can't, do you feel unhappy?

Take a lesson from the woodpecker and don't worry about what you can't do. Find out what you *can* do. Can you run fast? Read books? Act friendly? Whatever it is, do your very best, and do it for the Lord.

SCRIPTURE: *God has given each of us the ability to do certain things well. Romans 12:6a, TLB*

REMEMBER: If others win prizes and you feel no good, Remember the woodpecker's knocking on wood!
Use your special talents as God says you should.

WHEN YOU PRAY: Thank God for the talents he has given you.

FROM A PROBLEM TO A PEARL

I's fun to walk along the seashore and pick up shells. You might find a clam shell that's shut so tightly you can't get it open. Oysters are kind of like clams. They're squishy little creatures who live in shells in the ocean. Oysters are good to eat, but some of them can do a special trick that makes them worth even more. They can turn a grain of sand into a beautiful pearl.

The sand gets inside the shell by accident. It feels bad to the little creature. The oyster takes care of the problem by covering the grain of sand with fluid. After a while, the sand and fluid turn into a beautiful, valuable pearl.

Life has its little problems that bother us, the same way the sand bothers the little oyster. Sometimes things go wrong. Sometimes people say things that hurt us. But God tells us not to be mean in return. He wants us always to be kind and forgiving. That way He can help us make something good out of the bad situation—just like the oyster does.

When something or somebody bothers you, ask God to help you make something good out of it.

SCRIPTURE: *And we know that in all things God works for the good of those who love him, who have been called according to his purpose.*
Romans 8:28, NIV

REMEMBER: Oysters don't fuss, they just get to work
Making pearls out of scratchy old sand,
God promises us He'll make good out of bad
If we'll trust Him to lend us a hand.

WHEN YOU PRAY: Ask God to help you turn a problem into something good.

BUSY BEAVERS

Did you know that a family of beavers can change a little stream into a little lake all by themselves? They do it by building a dam. The dam holds back the water so that it forms a pool.

The beaver begins by using its sharp teeth to chew through the trunk of a small tree. When the tree falls, the beaver pushes the wood into the stream. He swims along beside the floating log, pushing it to the place he wants the dam to be. Log by log, the dam grows.

Beavers stick to their work. Even though the job seems huge, they keep at it, one log at a time. Before you know it, they've created a beautiful lake.

Sometimes people have big jobs to do. If the job seems too big, it's easy to get frustrated and worried. But God tells us we don't need to worry. He promises to help us and take care of us. He wants us to trust Him and let Him help us one day at a time.

SCRIPTURE: *Don't be anxious about tomorrow. God will take care of your tomorrow too. Live one day at a time. Matthew 6:34, TLB*

REMEMBER: Beavers keep building one stick at a time,
And slowly their big job gets done.
God helps his children one day at a time,
As we work and keep trusting His Son.

WHEN YOU PRAY: Ask God to help you not to worry, but to do your best each day.